Awesome Animal Mandala Coloring Book

Coloring Book for Teens and Adults

by Patricia Azeltine

www.pkburian.com

ISBN 13: 978-1981794164
ISBN 10: 1981794166

Introduction

Coloring books are a great for stress relievers. And the Animal Mandala is a fun way to color animals. Let your creative side shine through! Let your imagination run wild, like these animals in the coloring book. There is no right or wrong coloring these pages, only relaxing fun time!

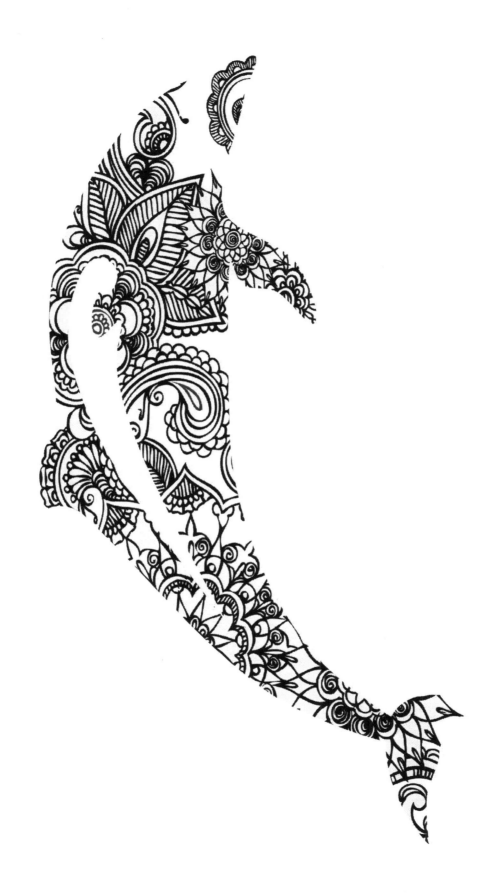

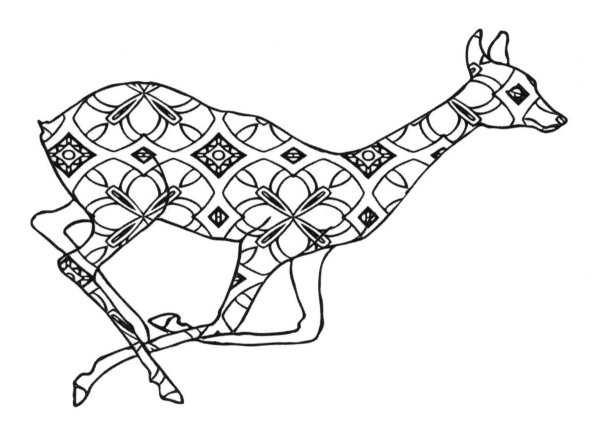

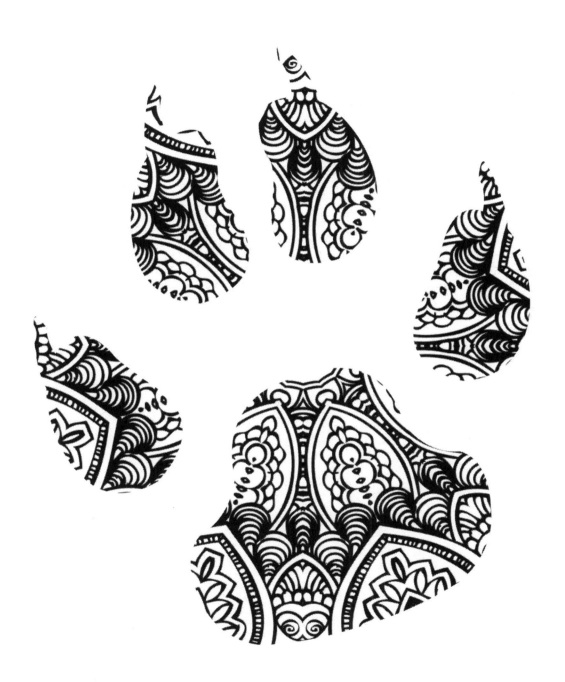

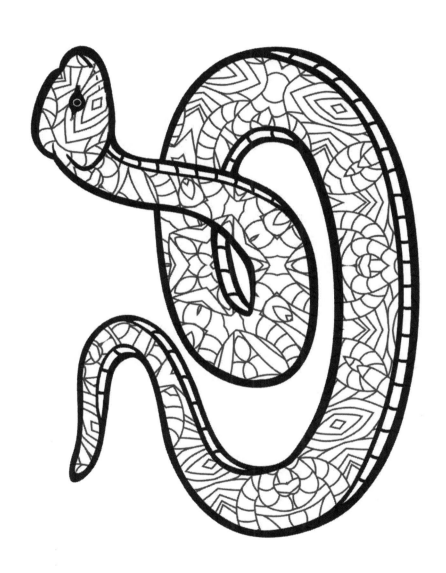

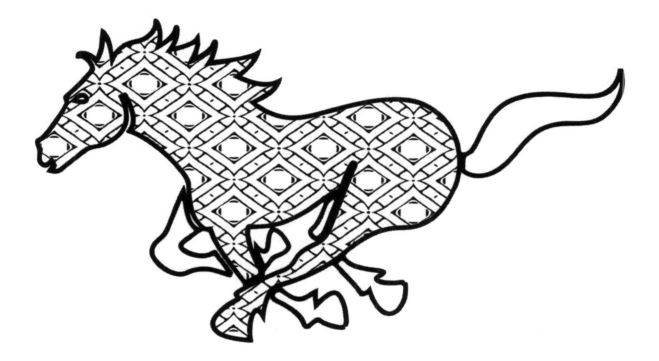

For more coloring fun for kids go to
http://www.pkburian.com.

Proof

Made in the USA
Columbia, SC
18 December 2017